Schiffer Publishing Ltd

4880 Lower Valley Road • Atglen, PA 19310

WITHDRAWN

CONDO

MAKEOVERS

CAMILLUS

INVENTIVE IDEAS FOR VERTICAL LIVING

E. ASHLEY ROONEY WITH CHARLENE KEOGH AND JULIE LINEBERGER

Other Schiffer Books by E. Ashley Rooney:
Green Homes: Dwellings for the 21st Century,
ISBN 978-0-7643-3033-9

Retreats to Retirement: Dream Homes to Reality,
ISBN 978-0-7643-2339-3

Tree Houses Reimagined, ISBN 978-0-7643-5150-1

Shingle Style Architecture for the 21st Century,
ISBN 978-0-7643-3551-8

LEEDING the Way, Domestic Architecture for the Future:
LEED Certified, Green, Passive & Natural,
ISBN 978-0-7643-4925-6

Designed by Justin Watkinson
Type set in Univers LT Std/Minion Pro/Zurich Lt BT

Front cover: RS3 Design (Photo by Michael Butler)
Back cover: Robert M. Gurney FAIA (Maxwell MacKenzie
   Architectural Photography)
ZeroEnergy Design (Eric Roth Photography)

ISBN: 978-0-7643-5130-3
Printed in China

Published by Schiffer Publishing, Ltd.
4880 Lower Valley Road
Atglen, PA 19310
Phone: (610) 593-1777; Fax: (610) 593-2002
E-mail: Info@schifferbooks.com
Web: www.schifferbooks.com

For our complete selection of fine books on
this and related subjects, please visit our website
at www.schifferbooks.com. You may also write for
a free catalog.

Schiffer Publishing's titles are available at special
discounts for bulk purchases for sales promotions or
premiums. Special editions, including personalized covers,
corporate imprints, and excerpts, can be created in large
quantities for special needs. For more information,
contact the publisher.

We are always looking for people to write books on
new and related subjects. If you have an idea for a book,
please contact us at proposals@schifferbooks.com.

Contents

Foreword

RENOVATING CONDOS

Julie Lineberger

Condo makeovers is a timely subject for people across the age and career spectrum. Many Americans who validated their success with large homes and gardens are aging. They wish to take advantage of all the amenities and activities that cities have to offer. With access to theater, food delivery, and concierge services, and without the responsibility of building and grounds maintenance, baby-boomer buyers see condos as an attractive option. The smaller living space becomes more finely tuned: possessions are culled, leaving the crème de la crème for the new home.

On the other end of the spectrum, condos are an increasingly attractive option for young professionals who are building careers. But these units are not always a smaller or less expensive alternative to single-family homes. August 2014 saw the most expensive apartment ever sold: $400 million for a 35,500-square-foot penthouse in Monaco. Although this is an extreme example, it reflects the desirability of well-placed condos and apartments.

Space is at a premium in urban areas and continues to increase in both value and demand. We hear of apartments in Paris, London, Tokyo, Rio, Boston, San Francisco, Seattle, and New York being handed down from generation to generation. Lesser-known cities such as Ann Arbor are having an apartment/condo building boom driven by calls for luxury housing for working professionals. Such projects routinely offer amenities such as a Zen garden, yoga patio, fitness center, and large common area with a game room available to all residents, including those in the ten-percent affordable units that many cities require in such buildings. In stacked housing, interior spaces need to flow and must be precisely designed within the confines of common walls and flooring. This rigor must be brought to every decision.

In renovating a condo, the basis for any decision is its intended use. A successful approach considers whether it is a primary or secondary residence, the expected duration of ownership, goals for long-term enjoyment versus short-term profit, and so on. Not all upgrades are created equal. Some add luxury without increasing worth. A spa bathroom with Italian marble does not matter a hoot if the rooms are dark or the floor plan is awkward. Beyond those broad brush strokes, keep in mind a few basic principles.

Kitchens are the heart of any home. Kitchen remodels return ninety percent of costs on average, making them one of the most valuable condo improvements, according to *Remodeling* magazine's 2015 "Cost vs. Value" report. However, major kitchen remodels don't return quite as much as mid-range and minor kitchen remodels. Most buyers won't pay extra for a built-in Sub-Zero refrigerator, imported tile, or designer faucets when quality mid-range kitchen features will do.

Appliances and cabinets are the most expensive items to replace, but they are usually worth it. If a kitchen is outdated, a new cooktop, stove, and refrigerator are solid investments— sellers recoup nearly every penny spent on appliances.

Bathrooms add resale value with updated counters, new faucets, good cabinetry, and hardware. Sparkling sinks and counters inspire "ahhs." Granite, marble, solid-surface stone composites, concrete, and stainless steel are some of the possibilities. When done well, less expensive options such as ceramic tile, soapstone, wood, butcher block, and laminates also impress. Buyers look for contemporary flooring (especially hardwood), room-enhancing light fixtures, and sufficient storage in the form of well-designed built ins.

How long domestic life will be disrupted during a renovation is always a concern for clients. The answer depends on defining a clear scope of work and avoiding a well-known affliction called "project creep."

For example, one of my clients wanted to paint a living room. Since the work was being done, he decided to take down the drop ceiling. Once the ceiling was removed, he imagined creating a sculptural element within the ceiling. Ultimately, his plan to repaint the living room turned into a major living room upgrade. The client was pleased with the outcome, but clear communication regarding each step was essential. The most important thing, however, is to create a living environment you enjoy. A primary home, even if it is an apartment or condo, is not a financial investment. It is an investment in yourself and your family.

Whatever one's situation, it is fun to peruse the variety of ways people develop, construct, accessorize, and live in their condominiums or apartments. The variety of tastes and ideas Ashley Rooney curated for this book offers hours of exploration and "oh, wow" moments. Enjoy!

—Julie Lineberger is principal of LineSync Architecture, an award-winning firm in Wilmington, Vermont, and a business management consultant.

Preface

ONE OF THESE DAYS

E. Ashley Rooney

I've never lived in a condo, but maybe one of these days I will sell my big old house and downsize into a smart little condo on a Florida beach, or maybe in New York, where I can enjoy the finest theater, culture, and food.

Condos seemed to suddenly appear in the 1960s, but the idea can be traced to nearly two centuries BCE. Many ancient civilizations had them. When Europeans decided to defend their cities by building walls around them during the Middle Ages and living space became scarce, people began to own rooms or floors of dwellings. It was much better to live in a small space inside the city walls than outside them!

In the late nineteenth century, Americans could purchase apartments in owner-occupied buildings known as home clubs. Home clubs gave birth to cooperatives, where the residents owned shares according to the size of their apartments.

Eventually, the scarcity of land near big cities, a growing population, and the cost of real estate led to the concept of private apartment ownership. Like a homeowner, a condominium buyer could purchase a unit that they could make theirs, and it could increase in value.

Florida developers were some of the first to jump on the bandwagon. They saw that these multi-unit buildings would appeal to an aging population who no longer wanted to deal with maintainance but wanted to own their home. Seeking the fun of city living, many aging boomers now sell their snow shovels and lawnmowers and head for condos in cities. Urban condominiums and condo-hotels allow them to enjoy the arts, food, and building amenities.

But condos and apartments aren't just for an aging population. Their sound economic value makes them popular among families and young professionals who work in the city. Overseas investors who want that annual vacation in a big American city also like condos.

Julie Lineberger addresses some of the issues involved in condo renovation in the foreword, and in the introduction, Charlene Keogh describes the design opportunities and challenges of this type of living space. The projects included show how architects and designers creatively solved those challenges to give their clients the inspiring spaces they desire. I hope you'll enjoy this peek into condominium buildings from the Watergate to Tribeca, and from Beacon Hill to San Clemente, California.

Acknowledgments

A big thank you to Charlene Keogh and Julie Lineberger for their expertise and wisdom in helping to shape this book.

—E. Ashley Rooney

Many thanks to the real estate agents, co-op and condominium board members, condominium managers, mortgage brokers, contractors, and friends throughout the country who gave me excellent information. I extend my heartfelt thanks to Rochelle Crespi, Greg Gaske, Janie Molster, Phyllis Quinn, Dianne Rosenbluth, Michael Shapot, Jay Spellmon, Herb Stein, Nancy Vernon-Burke, Corinne Vitale, and Lisa Wong.

—Charlene Keogh

Introduction

LIFE IN THE CITY

Charlene Keogh

American cities are experiencing a renaissance of sorts. According to the Census Bureau, 2013 saw 2.3 million more people living in metro areas and their surrounding dense suburbs than in 2012—a shift that's been increasing since the economy began recovering in 2010. Condominiums and cooperative buildings are burgeoning around the country, not just in major cities like New York, Chicago, and Miami, but also in smaller cities such as San Francisco, Nashville, and Chapel Hill, North Carolina. Modern condos and co-ops are rushing to include amenities such as "hotel" space for house guests, gyms, wine cellars, maid service, restaurants, and even pet spas—all the things that make life easier. Families with young children are doing what they can to stay in cities and towns. Urban planners are creating greenbelts with parks, playgrounds, and bike paths for outdoor recreation spaces. Both millennials and empty-nesters want to be near the culture and energy cities offer.

As a result, those legal entities, condominiums and cooperatives, have become more important than ever. Cooperative apartments came into being in the early part of the twentieth century, but became really popular in the 1980s, with cities seeing many conversions. A co-op apartment means that the owner doesn't actually own the physical apartment; he or she owns building shares in proportion to the size and desirability of the apartment. A condo owner does own the physical space, and the rules for condos can favor those who want a part-time pied-à-terre or are coming from abroad. Of course, there are pluses and minuses to each form of ownership depending on the buyer's needs.

Creating a home in this kind of building has specific challenges. In a co-op or a condo when there is to be construction or renovation of any kind, plans must be submitted for approval to several entities before work begins. That means submittals to the building's board and the building's own architect, the

East 87th Street

Tribeca loft

city's building department, and possibly to a landmarks commission if the building is in a historic neighborhood. This can add a significant layer to the approval process. New York City's Landmarks Preservation Commission was created in 1965 following huge public outcry after the destruction of Pennsylvania Station to make way for construction of the current Madison Square Garden. The commission is responsible for protecting New York City's architecturally, historically, and culturally significant buildings by granting them landmark or historic district status, and regulating them once they are designated. It is the largest municipal preservation agency in the nation, but by no means the only one, as other cities have taken note. As a designer and a New Yorker, I believe these rules are necessary and have helped keep many historic buildings from being disfigured, or worse, torn down.

Consequently, a designer or architect working in a condo or co-op, in what is known as "vertical living," never starts with an empty page. What is being designed for a client must take into consideration both space restrictions and the legal ones mentioned previously. For example, a restriction known as "wet over dry" means a designer/architect can't normally put in a bathroom (or kitchen or laundry) unless there is an existing "wet" area below; plumbing stacks have to follow what's already there. Makes sense, doesn't it? As Paul Simon sang in 1973, "one man's ceiling is another man's floor." At this point, a design opportunity often appears, which can result in a more interesting and creative solution!

There can be other constraints, such as the daily hours that work is allowed to occur; projects that can only be done between Memorial Day and Labor Day; small freight elevators for loading supplies, cabinetry, and furniture; and narrow streets for construction vehicles. Of course, boards generally make rules to keep everyone in check so that neighbors don't have to endure constant construction. Simply put, good designers have to be good planners, and good contractors have to be good forecasters: potential problems, issues, orders, and deliveries have to be determined up front and carefully planned in order to maintain the project schedule. If timing gets off track, a client might have to wait a year before work can resume.

When starting a remodel, an architect or designer needs to understand the style of the building and its place in architectural history to guide the direction of the work. Is it a prewar (that is, pre-WWII) building, a 1950s white-brick building, a former factory, or brand-new? It is key to pay attention to what is already there for both aesthetic reasons (ceiling height, hallway space) and practical reasons (plumbing and electrical). A client and designer can then decide how much the building's historic period will influence decisions.

Sometimes we are faced with older apartments where all previous architectural details have been stripped away (that happened a lot in the 1960s and 1970s). And sometimes, in the older buildings, it can turn into an archaeological dig! Newer buildings, unfortunately, can mean shoddily built infrastructure that has to be upgraded. Fixing poor circulation flow from room to room, or creating a new open space to meet modern needs, adds to the "fix" possibilities.

For example, an apartment on East 87th Street had low, eight-foot ceilings that could not be made higher (page 7). To create the illusion of height, we used high-gloss white ceiling paint and polished stone floors. The opposite situation presented itself in a duplex Tribeca loft in an old factory building with twenty-foot ceilings (opposite). My design had to ensure that my client didn't feel lost in a cavernous space, yet provide enough space to hold large gatherings without feeling crowded. In both apartments, designing and choosing furniture to scale was paramount. *(Photos courtesy of Dan Muro, Fast Forward Unlimited)*

In any given city, a designer or architect has the chance to design for many different kinds of spaces, with all kinds of possibilities. As you will see, these possibilities are being applied in historic buildings, converted warehouses, plain old 1980s white boxes, and new modern buildings, with spectacular results. Enjoy reading—and looking!

—Charlene Keogh, ASID, CID, NCIDQ, is principal of Keogh Design Inc., New York. She graduated from Pratt Institute and had the privilege of working with George Nelson and Ulrich Franzen, who were early and continuous influences in her career.

53 Unique Residences
CetraRuddy Architecture

LOCATION: New York
SIZE: 280,000 square feet (unit sizes vary)
LANDSCAPE ARCHITECT: H. M. White
LIGHTING DESIGNER: Kugler Ning

Built in the nineteenth century as a seven-story bookbindery, 443 Greenwich is being restored and adapted into fifty-three residences. The design, inspired by original architectural details and the grand proportions of the existing structure, celebrates the original construction while introducing distinctive, crafted details that complement modern materials. The design emphasizes natural light through the use of large arched windows, double-height spaces, and views of the lushly landscaped courtyard.

Each residence has the open expansiveness of the lofts that are part of Tribeca's design heritage, echoing the industrial district's past. Generous, well-ordered spaces are laid out and proportioned to evoke an elemental beauty and inspire a serene, meditative state that belongs more to a sacred place than a place of busy industry. Allées of original wood columns and beams anchor each unit to the structure.

Custom artwork by Andrea Lilienthal hangs above an eighteenth-century Chinese lacquer side table. *Photo © Eric Laignel*

Suffused light brings grace to the great material presence of the building, whose many windows reveal the radiance of the nearby Hudson River.

The large kitchen pays homage to home with the warmth of an inviting central hearth. Reminiscent of cooks' kitchens in Normandy, it features a millwork wall of open shelving filled with dishes and personal collections in the informal manner of a farmhouse. Rustic white oak flooring complements the contemporary aesthetic of stainless steel, polished chrome hardware, and black stone countertops, all framing the Calacatta marble island centerpiece.

Material palettes, furniture, and fixtures reflect the design's pairing of historic and contemporary, rustic and refined.

The master bathrooms offer deeper moments of solitude. Bold materials, such as hand-selected specimen marble slabs set behind sculpted bathtubs, respond to the building's monumentality. Long, trough-like sinks add a "primordial" element, juxtaposed against the refined white marble and antique bronze detailing.

Cooper Square Loft
Desai Chai Architecture

LOCATION: New York

SIZE: 5,000 square feet

GENERAL CONTRACTOR: Giovannitti

STRUCTURAL ENGINEER: Donald Friedman, Attila Rona

MECHANICAL ENGINEER: Simon Rodkin Consulting Engineers

LIGHTING: Christine Sciulli Light + Design

AUDIOVISUAL: WTB Associates

The renovation of this L-shaped industrial loft maintains the sense of spaciousness and allows light to flow throughout. Spun aluminum domes define the dining area and hide drainage pipes coming from the roof. *Photos courtesy of Paul Warchol*

Large windows wrap the corner where
the living and dining areas intersect.

Light floods the entry corridor.

Dimmable xenon fixtures in the
domes create an even wash of light.

Light shines through the offset slats of wood and glass skin in the study and bath. The luminous wall system allows light to bounce into various rooms while screening direct views inside.

The kitchen, surfaced with anodized aluminum and glass, plays an important role in emitting and dispersing light. The variety of reflective, transparent, and translucent materials breaks up the surfaces while allowing for ample storage. A clear glass soffit exposes the air-conditioning ductwork and also acts as a large lighting feature. The cantilevered island welcomes all the activities of family life, from cooking and eating, to reading and working.

Operable portholes in the glass and wood-enclosed den and bathrooms allow for ventilation and visual connections.

Large, modular storage units act as spatial dividers and demarcate the three bedrooms at the rear of the loft. The units have storage inserts, much like steamer trunks, that can be opened up or closed completely.

Tribeca Skylight Penthouse
George Boyle Architect

LOCATION: New York
SIZE: 4,000 square feet
GENERAL CONTRACTOR: AJS/Matrix

This light-filled Tribeca penthouse looked up for inspiration and never looked back. The duplex/rooftop addition was conceived as a three-dimensional filter of light and sky views by way of overlapping slices in the roof, floor, and walls.

Cut away, the upper floor floats off the side walls to let sunlight/shadow paint the two-story spaces. This view, from the kitchen below, allows one to feel the sun, rain, snow, or night, while the openings from below hint at what is above.

Light from above and the sides
telegraphs down the stair opening to
the lower dining/living areas.

The upper floor, with its burnished concrete floor and glass guardrails, further emphasizes its connection to the sky.

To accentuate the lightness and sky above, cantilevered wood block steps reduce in thickness as they ascend.

A porous wall separates the master
bath from the borrowed scenery of
the garden shared by the master bath
and bedroom.

A continuous operable glass wall
opens to the ipe terrace and
skyline beyond.

Mount Snow Ski Condo
LineSync Architecture and Planning

LOCATION: West Dover, Vermont
SIZE: 1,111 square feet
FURNISHINGS: 2 Sisters Home Furnishings
GENERAL CONTRACTOR: Fred & Fred Jr. Builders

This top-floor condominium was perfect except for one thing: the neat perch over the kitchen, accessed by ladder, violated building code. The inspectors wanted this unsafe loft space removed, but the architects had another idea: rather than lose valuable sleeping area, why not access the loft and the other upstairs bedroom with a new stair bridge? *Images courtesy of CarolynBates. com*

A glass bridge (above right)—three-inch-thick pavers made by local artisans—creates a sense of separation and escape. Its locally fabricated steel grate was sandblasted and given an oil and wax coating, lending a soft, velvety pewter look that complements the home's warm wood tones. A wood soffit conceals uplights.

The main post for the perch was braced to provide extra roof support during heavy winter snows. Wood panels were joined like blocks to convey solidity to the post while hiding potential expansion and contraction cracks along the wood span. Hammered copper tiles lighten the blocks, and copper pipe trim plays off the stair railing.

The stairs were reconfigured to serve both the bedroom on the left and the loft on the right (an enclosed attic room in a previous life). Light floods the underside of the bridge, illuminating the foyer entrance. The copper stair rails were affordably sourced as ⅝-inch-diameter electrical grounding rods used in utility installations.

The perch sits above a refinished kitchen warmed by custom cabinetry and locally quarried Ashfield schist countertops. The custom handrail is a pair of stock railings with the bottom element flipped in a mirror image.

The kitchen's birchwood bar caps a
copper-tiled wall and copper foot rail.
Lighting inside each door turns the
cabinetry into illuminated
shadowboxes for
decorative stemware.

First Avenue Apartment
Mojo Stumer Associates, PC

LOCATION: New York
SIZE: 7,000 square feet
GENERAL CONTRACTOR: Tennis Planning/Automatic Group
ENGINEER: Kam Chiu
EXPEDITOR: Praxis Workshop Inc.

What began as two combined 2,300-square-foot apartments now encompasses three apartments joined by a main gallery that displays the client's art collection. The entrance contains a clean palette of white marble and dark stone, combined with white lacquer soffits and a macassar ebony sculpture stand with stainless steel inserts. *Photos courtesy of Mark D. Stumer*

A mechanically operated panel
opens and closes the kitchen
to the dining room.

In the kitchen, white lacquered cabinetry contrasts with the dark subway tile backsplash and custom stainless steel range hood.

On the 82nd floor, the living room's ten-foot-high curtain wall frames a spectacular view of New York City.

The media room is finished with sleek furnishings and cabinetry.

A custom wine room stores the client's large wine collection. Outside the glass enclosure, black and red furniture complements a dramatic light fixture.

The master bathroom has stunning views, even from the shower. Mosaic tiles and stainless steel cover the custom tub. The vanity features rectilinear vessel sinks and teak shelves for towel storage.

Apartment 24
Robert M. Gurney, FAIA Architect

LOCATION: Washington, DC
SIZE: 2,750 square feet
INTERIOR DESIGNER: Therese Baron Gurney
GENERAL CONTRACTOR: Added Dimensions

Built in 1928, this Spanish colonial apartment building in Washington's Kalorama Triangle Historic District is listed on the National Register of Historic Places. Interior spaces, including the main lobby and hallways, are ornate and elaborately detailed. The individual apartments are spacious and bright; however, the units were compartmentalized, greatly reducing the sense of space.
Photos ©Maxwell MacKenzie Architectural Photographer

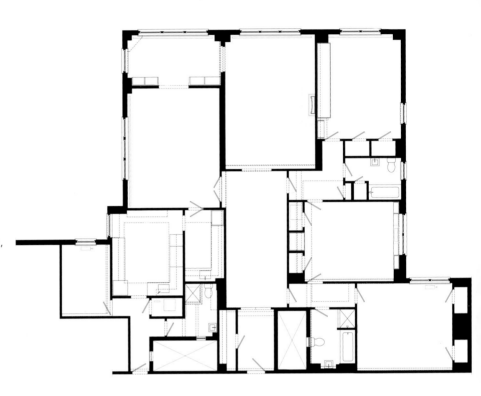

before FLOOR PLAN
0 2 4 6 8 10

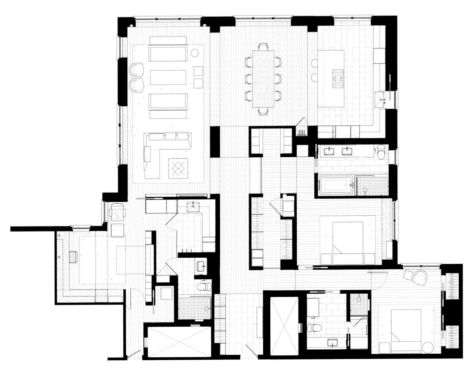

The gutted interior was reorganized within a framework of existing concrete columns and beams and electrical, plumbing, and mechanical infrastructure, creating a series of open, interconnected spaces filled with light. A central line of columns and beams defines the entry and main circulation gallery.

FLOOR PLAN
0 2 4 6 8 10

The view from the entry extends through the entire apartment. Gurney repositioned the kitchen, living, and dining spaces to receive maximum sunlight, while bedrooms and other secondary spaces occupy the interior.

Cabinetry and millwork are arranged in horizontal and vertical layers that define and unify spaces. The material palette—dark-stained oak flooring, white oak cabinetry and paneling, zebrawood, glass, and aluminum— unifies the spaces throughout.

Detailing is crisp and minimal, a foil
for the building's ornate lobby and
hallways. Translucent glass panels
have a diaphanous quality while
creating a subtle awareness of space
beyond. The reorganized floor plan
demonstrates how a landmark historic
building can continue to serve a
modern urban population.

Sky Loft
KUBE architecture

LOCATION: Washington, DC
SIZE: 1,300 square feet
GENERAL CONTRACTOR: Metrix Construction
GLASS: Gaithersburg Glass
MILLWORK: Mersoa Woodwork

A two-story loft with windows only in the front, a small kitchen, and scarce storage was transformed into a light-filled gallery in which to display the owner's extensive art collection. The living/dining area was enhanced by enlarging the opening in the floor above and replacing a drywall enclosure with a frameless glass railing. *Images courtesy of Greg Powers Photography*

To preserve the purity of the two-story
volume, KUBE concealed all ancillary
rooms (kitchen, bathroom, closets,
and staircase). The kitchen was
enlarged and can "disappear"
behind the sliding doors at left.

Decorative shelving can be exposed or hidden away.

The master bathroom is veiled behind
large frosted glass panels, visible from
the living room below.

View of master shower.

Storage solved: On the second floor,
white pivot doors conceal a line
of closets that runs the length
of the apartment.

Pied à Terre
A4 Architecture & Planning

....

LOCATION: Newport, Rhode Island
SIZE: 660 square feet

The gut renovation of this formerly dark and dank pied-à-terre overlooking Newport Harbor shows that luxury is more a by-product of quality than quantity. The makeover included a new kitchen, comfortable living area, spacious bedroom, laundry area, walk-in closets, luxurious master bath, and new powder room. Large sliding pocket doors were used to connect the main living space with the bedroom to make both spaces feel larger. Light colors and marbleized countertops help to reflect light and brighten the compact apartment.

West Side Loft
Office of Architecture

....

LOCATION: New York

SIZE: 3,000 square feet

GENERAL CONTRACTOR: Sohome

DESIGN COLLABORATOR: Push

KITCHEN SYSTEMS CONSULTANT: Fellini Designs

SHADES: Advanced Window
Coverings Associates

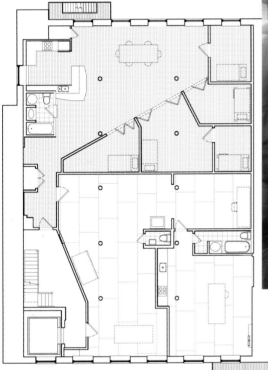

BEFORE

AFTER

Too often, "loft living" forces a compromise between Bohemian charm and personal privacy. The informal plan, ample natural light, and uninterrupted views of an open loft are typically at odds with the desire for private space and distinct bedrooms. This project embraces both, transforming one floor of a nineteenth-century landmark warehouse into a casual home for a young family. The new living area takes advantage of natural light and views from both ends of the deep floor plate without compromising privacy. Materials include custom walnut veneer millwork, wide plank walnut flooring, basaltina lavastone millwork countertops, and fireplace cladding. *Photos courtesy of Kishore Varanasi*

Gutting the previously labyrinthine space left only key structural elements, making possible a reciprocal relationship between public and private zones.

The kitchen system by Cucine Lube
includes Gaggenau appliances, Vola
kitchen faucets and fittings, and
lighting by Tech Lighting, Hera,
and Nippo.

Custom walnut millwork defines the
entry and frames the windows at each
end of the loft.

To further define space and accommodate various activities, the team designed a series of built-in accessories such as floating walnut multipurpose cabinetry, a cantilevered wet bar, and several full-height sliding and accordion panels. Service zones that house laundry and bathrooms on the left of the entry space are enclosed by full-height folding partitions with Hafele hardware.

Minimal walnut millwork detailing contrasts with the original white brick walls of the nineteenth-century factory.

A walnut workspace is concealed behind custom sliding doors. This workspace also acts as a thick partition between the open living area and the middle bedroom. Custom walnut pocket doors are fitted with Hafele hardware.

The jewel-box-like master bedroom holds a built-in platform bed, side tables, and custom walnut cabinetry with Hafele hardware.

Two large floating millwork pieces separate the entryway from the living/ family/wet bar area.

Translucent sliding panels offer easy access to kitchen supplies.

A partition system of shingled glass screens the master bathroom and study from view while allowing the exchange of light from adjacent rooms.

The upper portion of these rooms is a continuous glass skin that gives shape to the light. The structures act as beacons in the space, lighting it from above; they illuminate the ceiling plane and connect the flow of light in an otherwise dark interior.

Horizontal bands of glass catch the light and subtly diffuse it into the internal spaces, while emitting a soft glow at the corners of the loft.

White linear subway tiles bounce light around in the bath and echo the original white terra-cotta patterns in the relic structural columns.

A continuous shelf bisects a cutout in the shower wall.

Sycamore Penthouse
George Boyle Architect

....

LOCATION: Tribeca, New York City
SIZE: 2,200 square feet
GENERAL CONTRACTOR: J. Kemp Construction

A matrix of sliding panels allows
rooms to evolve or dissolve in this
duplex penthouse. The kitchen flows
into the dining/living area; the stairwell
draws daylight from the master
suite above.

Steamed sycamore, Douglas fir, white oak, natural-edge walnut, and pietra cardosa stone lend warm, bright notes. Storage and seating under the stair create a mud-room-like alcove.

Sliding panels can be positioned to create varying degrees of enclosure in the children's rooms and study.

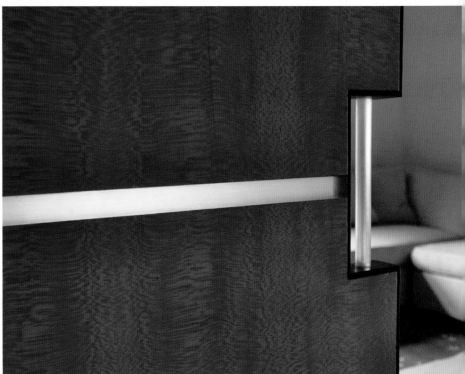

A strip of sanded plexiglass allows hints of light to escape from behind the door panels.

Quarter-sawn Douglas fir block
steps and sandblasted stainless steel
railings connect the main level to the
master suite and terraces above.

The ipe garden wall is zippered with sanded plexiglass blocks that fill with sunlight.

Facing west, the main terrace features a sliding barn-like panel (not shown). The graduated-slot privacy wall encloses the sitting area.

Watergate Apartment
Robert M. Gurney, FAIA Architect

LOCATION: Washington, DC
SIZE: 1,250 square feet
INTERIOR DESIGNER: Therese Baron Gurney, ASID
GENERAL CONTRACTOR: Added Dimensions and D. Anthony Beale LLC

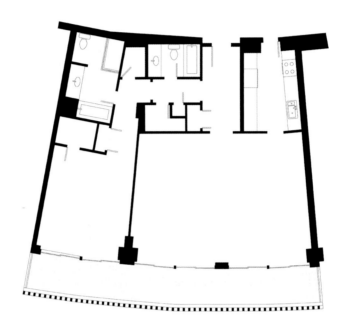

FLOOR PLAN - BEFORE

0   4   8

Designed by Italian architect Luigi Moretti, the Watergate complex was built between 1963 and 1972. It overlooks the Potomac River and is considered one of Washington's most desirable addresses.

Still in its original form, this unit's compartmentalized spaces and eight-foot, four-inch ceilings gave the perception of a low horizontal environment. *Photos ©Maxwell MacKenzie Architectural Photographer*

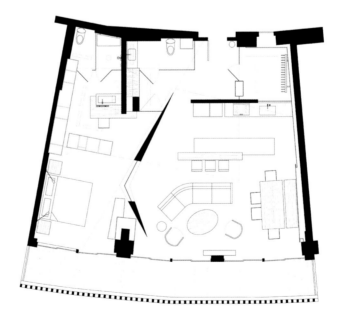

FLOOR PLAN - AFTER

0   4   8

The gut renovation included removing the flooring to the concrete slab and creating open living spaces oriented to views of the river and the landmark Francis Scott Key Bridge.

An angled plaster wall near the entry organizes the apartment and directs views along the river and toward the Key Bridge. Electrostatic glass in the wall allows both privacy and views into the living spaces from the bedroom. Strips of stainless steel are inset into the white terrazzo flooring to reinforce established geometries and floating ceiling planes.

A wine niche behind the kitchen
makes it feel larger.

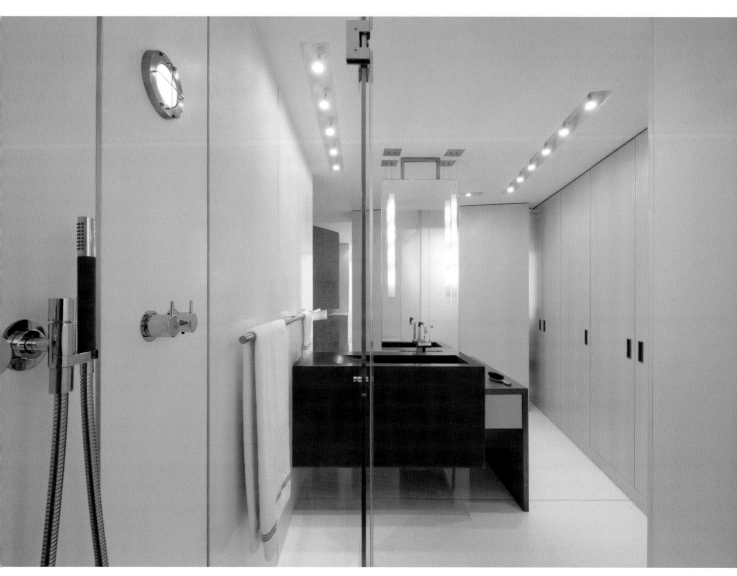

Forms and textures both unify and diversify the spaces. White terrazzo flooring becomes the stage for ribbed grain walnut wall paneling, white ash millwork, luminous glass walls, integrally colored charcoal plaster, aluminum, and black concrete.

Riverside Apartment:
An Answer to Tropical Storm Irene
LineSync Architecture and Planning

LOCATION: Wilmington, Vermont
SIZE: 775 square feet
INTERIOR DESIGNER: Interior Furnishings by Nona
GENERAL CONTRACTOR: Todd Gareiss

A so-called 100-year flood destroyed this below-street-level apartment in a mixed-use building on the Deerfield River. LyneSync's research into its rehab extended to every facet and fastening, resulting in a resilient design that responds to extreme weather patterns, down to its new bones.

The new floor plan replaces small, awkward rooms with a single great room that takes in the river view. Original posts and beams are now exposed, permitting inspection of key support structures in the future. The structural members also add scale and proportion to the linear space. *Images courtesy of John Sprung, Photographer*

The wood-framed walls and floors were ripped out. Shown here in the pre-furnished living room, interior walls are constructed of concrete blocks covered with Thinset tile adhesive, which provides an impermeable surface and lends a warm, handmade finish. The radiantly heated concrete slab flooring will dry quickly in future floods. The river-blue acid-stained finish was sealed so as not to absorb contaminated floodwaters.

To ensure adequate drainage in a
future flood, each room features a
one-way drain. The dark-stained
hardwood floor edge afforded better
continuous insulation and a more
stable finish than thin concrete over
the existing wood eight-by-eight-inch
sill. It also reflects the corrugated
metal wall panels. Their galvanized
finish is impervious, and the exposed
fasteners facilitate easy access to
wiring. Reflected light dances off
the metal wall surfaces, like the
reflections on the river waters.

The bedrooms were moved in order to maximize living space on the river side of the apartment. Large egress windows increase the natural light.

A single masonry wall divides the apartment into public and private halves. Interior transoms carry light from the river-facing side of the apartment into the bathroom and bedrooms. Wherever possible, services are ceiling-fed. Wires are rated for submersion, and mechanical equipment is placed upstairs above the flood level, along with a generator hookup.

The architect and builder devised windows that can be quickly removed and saved in a future flood. Exterior-grade, surface-mounted lighting replaced concealed fixtures that break easily and are difficult to remove.

Leather District Loft
Studio Luz

....

LOCATION: Boston
SIZE: 1,200 square feet
GENERAL CONTRACTOR: Aldor Corporation
MILLWORK: Mystic Millwork, Infusion Furniture

Formerly a compartmentalized warehouse loft, this Leather District condo was reorganized as a simple rectangular box with the "wet' areas stationed against the long wall that houses the plumbing core. The dining table is a seven-foot cantilever that can seat the couple, host a party of six, or disappear into the island. Stops for different settings allow the table to be locked into place. In the living room, dark sliding panels conceal the television cabinet and wine collection. To give the bedroom a bit more separation, the architects raised it on a platform, with bookshelves nested beneath that face the living room.
Photos courtesy of John Horner

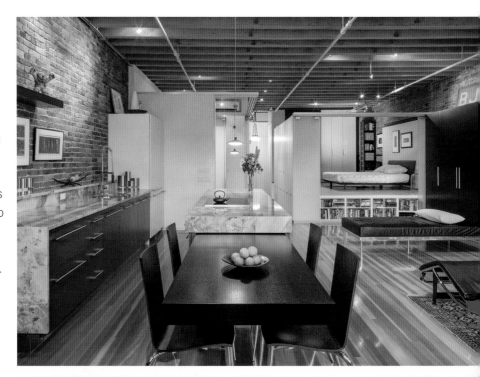

An open kitchen, dining, and living area are naturally lit by three arched windows, while the adjacent private rooms—a small office/guest room, master bedroom, and bath—operate on the scale of large furniture pieces.

The firm reinvented the drywall partitions with room divisions that are flexible and diffuse. Each room is fitted with a combination of translucent sliders and storage walls that stop short of the ceiling, preserving a sense of the entire loft and letting the clients choose different levels of privacy.

The bedroom's deep red closet is made of MDF with a pigmented varnish similar to the spray finish used on cars. The closet's center bay on the opposite side, facing the entry hall, is used as a coat closet.

Clad in fiberglass with an epoxy resin, the bedroom platform and steps read as a monolithic slab.

View from the office/den. The architects preserved the character of the loft's materials—heavy timber beams, brick walls, wood floors. Damaged Douglas fir flooring was swapped out for new Douglas fir, which is fairly soft and will feel lived in as it ages.

Materials used in the bath
continue the sense of lightness
and translucency.

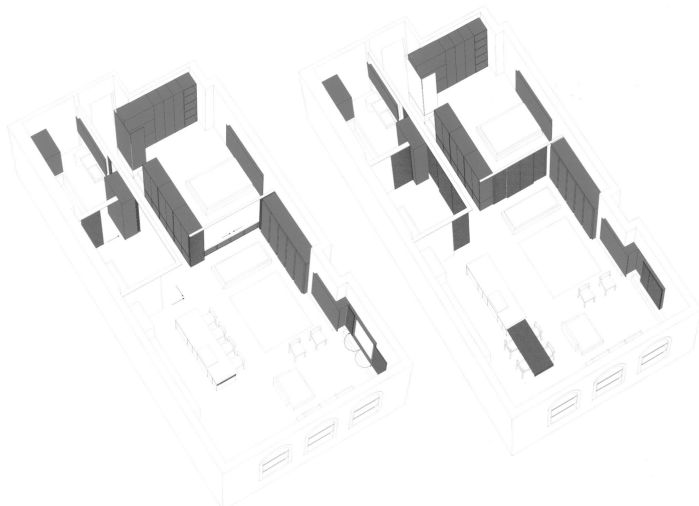

Perimeter Loft

Höweler + Yoon Architecture

LOCATION: Boston
SIZE: 1,800 square feet
GENERAL CONTRACTOR: Evergreen Group

In this postwar penthouse apartment in Boston's historic Back Bay, a single open living room and kitchen replaced a series of bedrooms along the south-facing perimeter. The master bedroom is adjacent. *Photos courtesy of Höweler + Yoon Architecture*

A pivot door to the master bedroom (with red chair) allows the sunny perimeter to be opened up.

The new master bathroom replaced two small bathrooms.

A second bathroom, at the center of the apartment, borrows light from a new skylit stairwell to the roof terrace. The stairs cascade down and transform into a bench and display area at the entrance.

The kitchen's material palette includes White Fantasy quartzite slab counters and white lacquered millwork. The pickled white oak flooring complements the other surfaces and gives the apartment a light and airy feel.

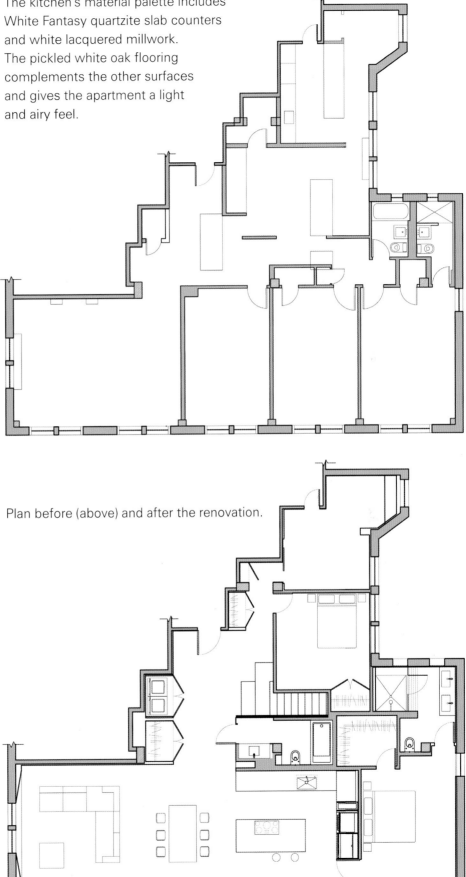

Plan before (above) and after the renovation.

West Village Apartment
Mojo Stumer Associates, PC

LOCATION: New York, New York
SIZE: 9,450 square feet
GENERAL CONTRACTOR: Built Rite Contracting
MEP ENGINEER: Stanislav Slutsky, PE, PC
STRUCTURAL ENGINEER: Robert Silman Associates

Four apartments were combined into one duplex penthouse containing a living room, bar, lounge, dining room, kitchen, dinette, three bedrooms, gym, massage room, his-and-hers closets, his-and-hers studies, and four bathrooms. The entry hall features split-face stone walls. Shelving is lined with LED track lighting that washes the accent wall; custom Lalique glass panels create an entry focal point.
Photos courtesy of Mark D. Stumer

The entry hall's white Glassos engineered stone flooring flows into the living room, with its modern furnishings and red accents.

A custom stainless steel, glass, and lacquer staircase separates the dining and living rooms.

A terrace extends the kitchen outdoors. The floor plan is programmed with main living spaces on one side of the residence and private functions such as bedrooms and baths on the other. The architects paired the client-requested red cabinetry with white and stainless steel accents.

Macassar ebony wood detailing and dark St. Laurent marble lend a masculine feel to the study.

OPPOSITE PAGE: A sculptural table and light fixture bring the kitchen's contemporary detailing into the breakfast area.

Beige accents and lighted cabinetry soffits have a calming effect in the master bedroom.

Family Loft
ZeroEnergy Design

LOCATION: Boston
SIZE: 1,750 square feet
GENERAL CONTRACTOR: Ralph S. Osmond Company
KITCHEN: Clever Green Cabinets, Gaggenau
FIXTURES: Hansgrohe, Laufen, Aquabrass
FINISHES: Creative Materials, Neolith

A young couple starting a family purchased this two-story 1990s loft in Boston's South End. The renovation goal was to create a fresh look, increase functionality to accommodate a growing family, and add texture, scale, and utility. *Photos courtesy of Eric Roth Photography*

The kitchen was reconfigured with more storage, larger prep surfaces, and new energy-efficient Gaggenau appliances. White paneling wraps the abutting wall, creating a neutral and textured surface, and walnut paneling accents on the island, cabinetry recesses, and upper wall and ceiling contribute much-needed warmth and scale to the living space with its twenty-foot ceiling.

The fireplace area was re-envisioned
for improved aesthetics, scale, and
proportion. Former clutter-prone open
shelves are now clean, functional
cabinets, paired with a stone element
for added texture. The glass curtain
wall offers extensive natural lighting
and views. The dark hardwood floors
were removed, and the concrete
below was polished, creating a
durable, low-maintenance finish
that helps disperse the light.

New walnut stair treads lead to an
office perch and the master suite.
Surfaces built into the new railing atop
the stair create a functional work area
with a fantastic view and clear shot to
the play space below.

A folding glass door replaced the wall separating the master bedroom from the double-height living space. This step opened the bedroom to the living space while creating visual and acoustical privacy.

OPPOSITE PAGE: Built within the mezzanine railing, a work area overlooks the double height living space.

The reconfiguration of the master bathroom opened up the space by pairing a platform shower with a freestanding tub. The open shower, wall-hung vanity, and wall-hung toilet create continuous flooring and an expansive feeling.

A family member made the walnut dining table, which in turn inspired the use of walnut throughout the loft, including the stair treads. The Little People chandelier was customized by adding the suspended red figure near the base.

The entry area became an urban mudroom with ample storage, a small, clean workspace, and the possibility of serving as an overflow sleeping area. Glass block borrows natural light from the abutting corridor while maintaining privacy.

Naval Officers Club Condo Conversion
Robert M. Gurney, FAIA Architect

LOCATION: Washington, DC
SIZE: 3,250 square feet
INTERIOR DESIGNER: Therese Baron Gurney, ASID
GENERAL CONTRACTOR: Added Dimension and D. Anthony Beale LLC

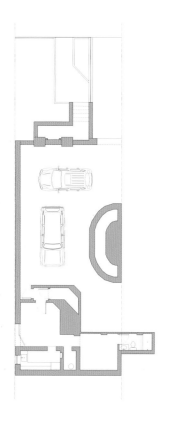

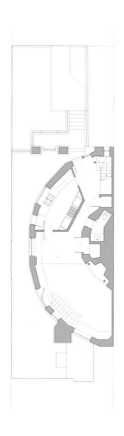

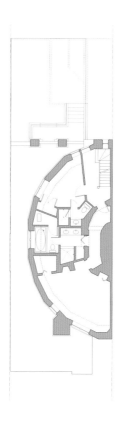

BASEMENT FLOOR PLAN
before

FIRST FLOOR PLAN
before

SECOND FLOOR PLAN
before

THIRD FLOOR PLAN
before

N
0   5   10   15

In 1944, the US Navy constructed a round, three-story brick building with below-grade parking near Washington's DuPont Circle neighborhood to serve as its Naval Officers Club. In 1990, the club was divided into two condominiums, each occupying half of the circular footprint. Because of the building's original central staircase and curving geometry, the reconfiguration resulted in small, oddly shaped rooms.

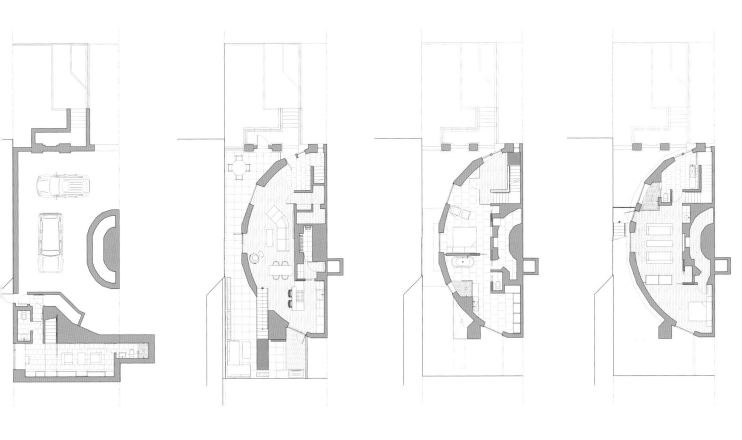

BASEMENT FLOOR PLAN

FIRST FLOOR PLAN

SECOND FLOOR PLAN

THIRD FLOOR PLAN

N

0   5   10   15

On the main level, new windows and
doors open to the terrace.

OPPOSITE PAGE: This unit was gutted
to the masonry bearing walls to open
it up. Most of the windows were
replaced with larger steel windows
and doors. *Photos ©Maxwell
MacKenzie Architectural Photographer*

OPPOSITE PAGE: A new glass bay strengthens the indoor-outdoor relationship, accommodating a relocated stair to the living space below the terrace and access to the parking area. A small section of the terrace, aligning with the glass bay, was removed and replaced with glass to provide natural light to the subterranean living area.

The redesign embraces the semi-circular footprint and makes the inhabitants aware of its unusual geometry from all vantage points. Dark oak flooring is a counterpoint to the crisp white walls punctuated with black steel window and door frames.

Throughout, glass, millwork, and oak
paneling define and enrich the spaces.

An outdoor room incorporates
cooking, dining, and seating areas.
Translucent glass panels and the
windowless walls of adjacent
buildings ensure privacy.

Timber Loft
George Boyle Architect

....

LOCATION: New York
SIZE: 2,200 square feet
GENERAL CONTRACTOR: J. Kemp Construction Inc.
METALWORK: Official LLC

Parts of the cast iron/wood timber structure of this nineteenth-century
landmark warehouse in Tribeca had been buried under decades of paint and
decay. The newly exposed structure determined the loft's layout and inspired
the use of "soft" industrial materials designed to fuse the excavated and new.
On one side of the loft is a main gallery with the living/dining/kitchen and
two-bedroom suite behind it; the powder room and master suite occupy
the opposite side.

An oversized corner walnut island anchors the kitchen. The two countertops are orthogonally joined: one side is laid on the "flat" while the other is set on the vertical, creating different edge thicknesses.

Central Park West
Chango & Co.

....

LOCATION: New York
SIZE: 2,300 square feet
GENERAL CONTRACTOR: Fox Force Five
MILLWORK FABRICATION: Mason Woodworks

This residence in the iconic 55 Central Park West building received a revamp that honors its historical integrity. The long, narrow living room was rearranged into distinct nooks that can be used for reading and lounging or a gathering place for a large group.
Photos by Jacob Snavely

Millwork wall cabinets maximize storage and conserve living space. The living room is outfitted with a large cream silk rug, English rolled arm seating, linen and down pillows, a collage of modern and vintage artwork, and custom built-ins with blue backs. On the far left wall, two African petrified animal heads add interest. Tufted ottomans with modern silver trays are used as coffee tables.

A high-arm tufted blue velvet settee coexists with white cashmere cable-knit pillows, modern geometric prints, and a tripod lamp.

The oversized hallway was converted into an efficient dining room. Custom built-ins incorporated into the new dining area contain an upholstered banquette flanked by an illuminated bar and 200-bottle wine cellar.

A metal table is paired with a dark cowhide rug and classic wood and rattan chairs. Round metal and leather mirrors delineate the seating area and help visually expand the space. Sheer window treatments admit every drop of natural light that illuminates the powdery gray walls.

OPPOSITE PAGE: This master bedroom features an upholstered and studded navy headboard, zinc dressers used as nightstands, and a light-colored silk rug. Motorized window treatments in chambray blue soften the room and carry the blue details throughout. Crisp white linens are paired with large silk pillows, lending the ambience of an English clubhouse.

Downtown Boston Penthouse
Haddad Hakansson Design Studio

LOCATION: Boston

SIZE: 1,300 square feet

TORSO WALL SCULPTURE: Rainer Lagemann, sourced by DTR Modern Galleries, Newbury Street, Boston

LIVING ROOM SECTIONAL: BoConcept

KITCHEN: Liebherr refrigerator; Miele induction cooktop, oven, hood, and dishwasher; Pennville Custom Cabinetry

Bordering Boston's South End, this condo is a five-minute walk to Boston Common. Built in the early 2000s, the two-bedroom, two-bath interior was given a contemporary overhaul and décor that reflects the owners' extensive travels. *Photos by Shelly Harrison Photography*

The staircase chandelier, with its strands of curled iron (Graffiti by Corbett Lighting), reflects light from all directions and draws the eye to the city views.

The sweeping curved staircase and two-story window wall define the entry. A small area under the stairs is the perfect place to tuck in a bistro table and stools. Bold art balances the impact of the sweeping views.

Downtown views are all the more dramatic at night, when the airy dining room transforms into a moody, sparkling space for entertaining. Sheer draperies and low-back chairs frame the skyline.

The sleek European-style kitchen leads to a terrace.

Plush carpeting, silk wallpaper, and luxury bedding transform the modestly sized master bedroom into a calm retreat.

Custom cabinetry in the home office/
guest room cleverly wraps the full-
height window (making it perhaps too
easy to spend time staring off into
space). Abstract art provides a pop of
color that complements the vibrancy
of the surroundings.

There is ample terrace space to relax
and soak up the buzz of Boston.

A crisp blue and white color scheme counterpoints the intense heat of Florida's coast. The designer applied Phillip Jeffries Luxe Linen metallic wallcovering to each square of the coffered ceiling to add sheen and texture overhead. A dark coffee table anchors the space, and a window seat between the bookshelves expands seating options.

Ceiling millwork defines the dining area and supports a linear chandelier. The dining banquette conserves floor space and blends with the ocean view. Hartmann & Forbes roman shades are fabricated with a material that appears wet and sparkling, like the ocean.

A dark-stained windowed frame contrasts with the white color palette and separates the kitchen and foyer. The partitioned glass panels are in a sliding track that allows the owner to serve food from the counter. The base of the unit is white on the kitchen side and dark on the foyer side, with paneled storage. Facing it across the foyer hall is a white ceiling-height built-in that offers both closed storage and a glassed area for display.

The master suite's coral accents were inspired by a favorite piece of artwork on the wall. Double pocket doors open to the lanai.

Gotham Views
Higgins Design Studio

LOCATION: New York
SIZE: 900 square feet
COUNTERTOPS: Caesarstone #2003 Concrete
BATH PORCELAIN TILE: Daltile CL65 City Lights

A welcoming sanctuary for the owners, transplants from Australia and New Zealand, this apartment provides a relaxed setting for entertaining out-of-town friends and family. A small alcove adjacent to the kitchen was converted into an inviting sitting area encircled by views of the city and East River. In contrast, oversized photographs of polar bears express the clients' bond with wildlife and wilderness environments. The built-in armless sleep sofa provides cushy lounge seating and accommodates overnight guests, while the drapery creates privacy and disappears into the wall when not in use. The boldly striped flatweave rug and mix of accent pillows set a fun, casual tone. *Photos courtesy of Anastassios Mentis Photography*

Higgins opened the kitchen to the adjacent living space so that the cook can socialize with guests. The linear pendant fixture provides ambient light, supplementing under-cabinet and recessed downlights. LED lighting highlights the grid of white lacquer panels beneath the front countertop.

The kitchen is designed for busy professionals who like to entertain informally. Its materials—custom white lacquer upper cabinets, figured gray sycamore lower cabinets, charcoal-stained rift-cut oak flooring, stainless steel appliances, and quartz countertops—blend seamlessly with the style of the adjoining areas.

The living area is open to the kitchen and sitting area. Its neutral tones and textures are punctuated with accents of bright turquoise and green. On the wall are wildlife photos taken by the clients during their travels. Wall-mounted linear fixtures wash the walls, providing ambient illumination.

The master bedroom is a haven high above the city. The built-in wall unit provides storage along the entire wall. The unit's figured gray sycamore finish creates interest but maintains a quiet tone.

With an accent wall of aqua glass mosaic tiles, the shiny white master bathroom is a sparkling oasis. Carrara marble tops the custom built-in white lacquer vanity with drawers. The built-in mirrored medicine cabinet provides a full wall of hidden storage. The mirrored doors and glass shower screen contribute to the open feeling.

Del Mar Loft
James Glover Residential and Interior Design

LOCATION: San Clemente, California

SIZE: 729 square feet

GENERAL CONTRACTOR: James Glover Residential and Interior Design

When they downsized to a smaller loft condo near the ocean, the clients requested a seamless living environment connected to the outside patio and ocean views. James Glover chose a light-colored material palette to enhance the natural light and removed walls to create flowing living space. *Photos courtesy of Allen Carrasco*

Wood flooring, white walls, and a
Calacatta marble countertop refine
the space and reflect light.

In the shower, limestone from Burgundy, France, creates a spa-like bathing experience.

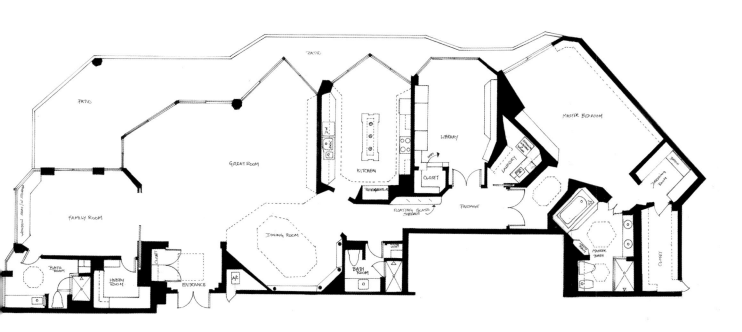

East 87th Street
Keogh Design Inc.

....

LOCATION: New York

SIZE: 3,000 square feet

GENERAL CONTRACTOR: Peter DiNatale & Associates

CUSTOM CABINETRY: Scanga Architectural Woodworking

CUSTOM RUGS: Carini Lang

CUSTOM SOFAS: Keogh Design Inc.

DEN SOFA/COFFEE TABLES: Ligne Roset

DINING TABLE AND CHAIRS: M2L

The apartment had an awkward entrance, strangely aligned soffits, and low ceilings. The renovated foyer became sleek and interesting with wood paneling, a mirrored wood wall above a built-in shelf and cabinet, and a sliding frosted-glass door that hides the kitchen entrance. A piece of antique tiled artwork is embedded into the wall and illuminated.
Photos courtesy of Dan Muro, Fast Forward Unlimited

Cabinetry-lined walls create a clean background to the living space. The framed mirror hides a flat-screen TV. Angled cabinetry incorporates an existing structural column and beam.

In addition to a TV room/den and workspace, this room can become a dining room when the coffee tables are raised to dining height, seating twelve. The embossed-leather banquette is designed to be comfortable for both lounging and dining. The frosted-glass sliding wall can be opened to the living room or closed for privacy. A curved desk and soffit resolved the problem of an awkwardly angled soffit enclosing the beam.

Another example of a multipurpose space, this room is a library, wine tasting room, and guest room. The sofa folds down into a guest bed.

The bedroom was given stipple-painted walls, a Carini Lang silk rug, and cabinetry that provides storage and hides the HVAC.

The bedroom's frosted glass doors admit light to an interior bathroom. Wood paneling conceals a full wall of closets while adding visual interest.

Aventura Loft Style Residence
RS3|Designs

LOCATION: Aventura, Florida
SIZE: 1,400 square feet
GENERAL CONTRACTOR: Critical Path Construction
MILLWORK: Arlican Wood
GLASS: MDV Glass

RS3 Designs created an extra bedroom in a former one-bedroom condo by closing off what was considered the dining area. Then they added glamor to the public spaces with a custom staircase made of glass railings, white laterals, and wenge steps. Wavy metallic wallpaper by ROMO was installed along the entire west wall leading from the foyer, through the staircase, and into the living room. The dropped ceiling has recessed lighting and hidden LED strips. *Photos courtesy of Michael Butler*

The living room is furnished with a white leather sofa, silver area rug, silver linen sheers, wall art from Michael Dawkins, and a custom ottoman/coffee table covered in snakeskin ROMO fabric.

RS3 designed the floating dining table fabricated by Arlican Wood. The black leather S chairs with metal chrome frames are from KOM; accent wall lighting is from Delta; and RS3 designed the artwork fabricated by Color House.

The kitchen continues the black and white theme with white quartz countertops by Santino Design and a cantilevered black glass bar top by RS3, fabricated by MDV Glass. The second bedroom is visible beyond the kitchen.

Custom glasswork closes off the second bedroom.

The master bedroom has a magnificent view. It is furnished with a custom white leather bed frame and headboard and a CasaDIO area rug from Rugs by Zhaleh. Flooring is white glass porcelain from Opustone; the ceiling is fitted with recessed lighting and hidden LED strips.

A frameless opening gives the master bath a grand view of the city. Arlican Wood fabricated the vanity's oak veneer; the sinks are from Farreys, and the white Thasos marble tile and countertop are from Opustone.

Monmouth Beach Condo
Sheila Rich Interiors

LOCATION: Monmouth Beach, New Jersey
SIZE: 1,700 square feet
GENERAL CONTRACTOR: O.C.C. and Associates
FINISH CARPENTRY: RLK Home Improvements

The owners, an artist and her husband, loved their ocean-view condo, but not its cookie-cutter layout that prevented her from displaying her large-format artwork. Adding to the problems, the cement ceilings made it difficult to add lighting. After the interior walls came down, bold blocks of color were added to discrete areas to balance and highlight the artwork. Here, the L-shaped purple wall backdrops a painting. *Photos by Peter Rymwid*

Crisp white ceilings contain recessed lighting, and their gray coffered interiors add a sense of depth. A hand-knotted custom rug complements the ceiling colors. The chandelier creates another focal point with its square glass beads and brass elements that contract with the nickel tones used throughout. Floating glass shelves with brass supports flank the resident artist's original artwork and display cherished collections. Motorized shades of sheer and solid fabric can be closed to protect furniture from fading, or raised, exposing the ocean view.

The renovation opened up a dark, narrow hallway. Soffits were added to the cement ceiling to accommodate recessed lighting. Previously, a full wall closed the kitchen island in the foreground. The purple passion wall continues around the corner from the living room, enhancing the artist's work and delineating the open area between kitchen and hallway.

A support column was pressed into service with the addition of crown molding, an LED-lit shelf, granite countertop, and mounted TV.

The glass range hood's graceful arc adds beauty without bulk. Puffy glass tile in a silver and white brick pattern counterpoints the marble, metal, and glass mosaic in shades of black and silver. The mosaic wraps the countertop, creating a horizontal flow. Pocket doors enclose the laundry closet, which houses a stacked washer/dryer.

The artist's work takes center stage in the den/guest room. A lamp made of plumbing fixtures sits atop a table whose three large drawers serve as additional storage space for overnight guests.

A floating vanity and mirrored wall make the narrow dressing area feel brighter and more spacious. A section of the floor was cut out and inlaid with the same marble tile used in the master bathroom. The center drawer in the vanity, which provides an extra sink, has a unique hand-painted glass knob. The ceiling fixture matches the one in the master bath.

In the master bedroom, a built-out dressing area and linen closet form a niche for the deco-style vanity and mirror. The table lamp—a cherished family heirloom—adds an eclectic touch to the Wedgwood-blue room. A blue wool leopard print runner completes the look.

Prewar Upper West Side Apartment
Chango & Co.

LOCATION: Upper West Side, New York
SIZE: 2,300 square feet
GENERAL CONTRACTOR: Reece Restoration

This seven-room prewar apartment next to Riverside Park was redesigned as a cooperative family space, a playful province for three children, and an eclectic, sophisticated sanctuary for the adults. *Photos by Jacob Snavely*

The home combines elements typical of prewar New York apartments: traditional English furniture, unlacquered antique brass fixtures, and large patterned wallpapers, but reinterpreted with the ease and whimsy that personifies this family's approach to life. Classic elements and furnishings were given a color palette of blues, salmon-coral, and chartreuse greens that complement the architectural era of the home and the strawberry-blonde hair of the residents. The redesign included new built-ins, slipcovered rolled arm furnishings, and brass hardware and light fixtures.

Built-ins contain the abundant collection of books and belongings while providing yet another opportunity for color through the use of cool blue cabinet backdrops and curated artwork and sculptures.

Two book-lined rooms flank the dining room: one is a crafts room and study for the children; the other is a lounge and library for the adults. Everyone can intermingle or inhabit their own space. The parents can live like grown-ups, and the kids are not forced to grow up too quickly.

The foyer introduces the blue and chartreuse color scheme used throughout.

The children enjoy playful quarters decked out with chalkboard-painted bookshelf backs and colorful accessories.

Peaceful High-Rise
Higgins Design Studio

....

LOCATION: New York
SIZE: 1,500 square feet
COUNTERTOPS: Silestone Amarillo Sand
KITCHEN AND BATH FITTINGS: Dornbracht Meta.02

The gallery-like foyer sets the tone for this condo, designed as a tranquil refuge and fundraising space and to showcase the client's art collection. The foyer's dropped ceiling has an illuminated recess that mirrors the shape of the seating area below it. Low, natural maple custom cabinets line the room, providing abundant storage and counter space for entertaining. *Photos courtesy of Anastassios Mentis Photography*

The flexible layout of the living/dining area works equally well for an intimate dinner for two or a cocktail party for twenty. The neutral color palette, with its range of tones and textures, creates a low-key backdrop, allowing guests and artwork to shine. The gauze-like linen Roman shades filter bright sunlight. The expanse of wool sisal carpet enhances the open feel and flexibility of the space.

Maple cabinetry, stainless steel appliances, and quartz countertops blend seamlessly with the materials of the adjoining areas. The classic artichoke pendant light above the table defines the dining area.

Lofty city views enhance the clean lines and play of textures in this contemporary home office tucked into a quiet corner.

High-Rise Beach Retreat
Pineapple House Interior Design

LOCATION: New Smyrna Beach, Florida
SIZE: 2,700 square feet
GENERAL CONTRACTOR: Del Mar Construction

Removing walls opened the entire living and dining area of this condo to the magnetic ocean view. Its coffered ceiling continues the cottage-style wood detailing of the new entry, which also has a beach view. Flush overhead lighting virtually disappears at the intersection of the living-room ceiling trim. The dining room chandelier is airy and light so it doesn't compete with the sweeping view. Drapery panels hang in integrated pockets along the perimeter and can be adjusted for privacy and climate control.
Photos courtesy of Mon Amour Photography

Upper cabinets flanking the stove were removed to make the kitchen's dominant wall more appealing. Kitchen storage was quadrupled via a twelve-door ceiling-height pantry near the dining table. In the foreground, two existing sofas were recovered in the same fabric so they look identical. To allow viewing in all directions, swivel mechanisms were added to the client's club chairs.

The kitchen is a sparkling focal point
when eyes turn away from the ocean.
On the far right, the ebony unit
contrasts with the jewel-like tile in
mother-of-pearl tones on the kitchen
wall. This furniture-like piece, which
anchors the kitchen's shortest wall,
has a dish display on its upper
portion and a microwave/convection
oven below.

The ebony kitchen unit is balanced by a coordinated breakfast and beverage bar near the dining area. It offers a second sink, storage, refrigeration, and Miele coffee maker. The wine cooler and under-counter refrigerator are housed behind decorative metal screens.

One side of the kitchen island supports the back of a custom banquette. The formality of the client's six ornate, carved dining chairs is tamed with upholstered chair backs and a simple short seat skirt in a light geometric fabric.

To create workspace, the designers incorporated a file cabinet under the dining room banquette, allowing the table to double as a desk. A plug next to the file drawer accommodates power cords.

The wall between the bedroom and bathroom was removed, allowing light and air to pour in from the sliding glass doors opposite the bathroom. The natural light and circulating fresh air significantly changed the personality of the formerly dark, tunnel-like master bath. A closet encloses the toilet at the far end of the wet area. Repurposing the client's writing desk as a vanity adds refinement to the integrated area.

A playful guest room provides lodging for the homeowner's grandchildren. The custom nautical-themed bunk bed sleeps five comfortably with one twin and two queen mattresses—one on a trundle. Portholes in the bookshelf visually link the bunk bed with a small lounging platform, which keeps guests from feeling hemmed in.

Oversized rope on the lounging platform supports the nautical theme. The lounge cushion is a removable outdoor terry cloth fabric with outdoor fill so swimmers can come straight from the pool or beach and relax without worrying about wet suits. Dock cleats serve as an unobtrusive ladder.

Resources

A4 Architecture and Planning
320 Thames Street
Newport, RI 02840
www.a4arch.com

CetraRuddy Architecture DPC
530 Canal Street #2E
New York, NY 10013
www.cetraruddy.com

Chango & Co
793A Willoughby Avenue
Brooklyn, NY 11206
718-455-2000
www.chango.co

Desai/Chia Architecture
37 West 20th Street, #710
New York, NY 10011
www.desaichai.com

George Boyle Architect PLLC
180 Duane Street
New York, NY 10013
www.gbarch.com

Haddad Hakansson
PO Box 614
Belmont, MA 02478
www.haddadhakansson.com

Higgins Design Studio LLC
55 E. 9th Street
New York, NY 10003
www.higginsdesignstudio.com

Höweler + Yoon
150 Lincoln Street, 3A
Boston, MA 02111
www.howeleryoon.com

James Glover Residential & Interior Design
103½ Avenida Del Mar
San Clemente, CA 92672
www.jamesglover.com

Keogh Design Inc.
180 Duane Street
New York, NY 10013
www.keoghdesign.com

KUBE architecture
1700 Connecticut Ave., NW, Suite 301
Washington, DC 20009
www.kube-arch.com

LineSync Architecture
14 Castle Hill Rorad
Wilmington, VT 05363
www.linesync.com

Mojo Stumer Associates (MSA)
14 Plaza Rd.
Greenvale, NY 11548
www.mojostumer.com

Office of Architecture (OA)
612 Degraw Street, FL2
Brooklyn, NY 11217
718-643-0371
Email: aniket@oa-ny.com
Website: www.oa-ny.com

Pineapple House Interior Design
190 Ottley Drive, NE
Atlanta, GA 30324
www.pineapplehouse.com

Robert M. Gurney, FAIA Architect
5110 MacArthur Blvd. NW
Washington, DC 20016
www.robertgurneyarchitect.com

RS3 Designs
1 NE 40th St. Ste 103
Miami, FL 33137
www.rs3designs.com

Sheila Rich Interiors
1 Channel Drive, Unit 1009
Monmouth Beach, NJ 07750
www.sheilarichinteriors.com

Studio Luz
21C Wormwood Street
Boston, MA 02210
www.studioluz.net

ZeroEnergy Design (ZED)
156 Milk St. Suite 3
Boston, MA 02109
www.zeroenergy.com

Index